Beyond the Waves

A Deep Insight to the World Around Us

Pritam Kumar Roy

BookLeaf Publishing

India | USA | UK

Made with ❤ on the BookLeaf Publishing Platform
www.bookleafpub.in
www.bookleafpub.com

Acknowledgement

Well, writing each poem in this book required a combination of intense reflection and feeling. Every poem I wrote intended to shed light on the subject and I also tried to finish each one in a way that would allow readers to relate to the verses and understand the poem's main point. In terms of giving thanks, I want to thank my parents, closest friends, family and well-wishers. I also want to thank my teachers for teaching me to never give up on my writing abilities, no matter what occurs in life. Finally, just as importantly, I want to express my gratitude to God for being kind and giving me strength during my trying times.

Preface

As the title page implies, this book contains poems that one can relate to one's life and environment. The book is on similar lines as the previous edition titled *Wave of Thoughts: An Attempt Towards Social Diagnosis*. It's an effort to highlight some public health topics and societal problems through poems. This collection of poems includes some of my own experiences as well that have greatly aided my ability to think clearly. All the poems' language is primarily spoken words, which would help readers comprehend the context and extrapolate meanings out of it. At the end of each poem, there is a footnote that provides the meanings of any words that may be confusing. Moreover, another goal of these poems is to promote a healthy life as research shows that they calm people's brains and induce a soothing sensation in them. I hope that others will be able to understand and decipher the meaning behind each poem in this book.

1. Serenity of a Village Haat

The dawn marks the beginning of our bazaar
haat[1] giving an ecstatic[2] sight,

As our eyes go towards the stalls blooming
bright,

All the humming buzz is just a real delight,

Making us laugh and enjoy with great might.

That essence of local fryums[3] is too tempting,

Delicious sweets and drinks leave our hearts
beating,

Gathering of folks of all ages is scintillating[4],

Each sharing their own old stories sans[5] any
boasting.

Soon dusk looms near to make the sight gloomy,

Vendors of all kinds packing their shelves and counting money,

This one long day forms the spine of their life's tourney[6],

Towards their home, they begin their long journey.

....

[1] *a village fair*

[2] *joyful*

[3] *local snacks made by frying*

[4] *shining*

[5] *without*

[6] *life has been considered as a tournament*

2. Jubilation of a Village Life

Shadows sway[1] in the village lanes,

With each passing day amidst[2] the rains,

Wind whirling around and quirking the window panes,

The soothing happiness has countless gains.

As we gaze[3] towards the endless fields beyond infinity,

Nothing but pleasant it is to behold such serenity[4],

The greens saving us from all the calamity,

It's just nothing short of absolute divinity.

Soon the skies turn dark in the nick of time,

Villagers yawn their way to sleep in prime,

Leaving the shooting stars alone and wind to chyme,

With a ray of hope to begin next day quite sublime[5].

....

[1] *move to and fro*

[2] *in between*

[3] *look in a fixed direction*

[4] *calmness*

[5] *glorious*

3. A Space Nurturing Young Minds

Strolling[1] around a village, there's a structure nestled among the trees,

Where tiny little heads run around playing games with ease,

As the birds chirp around and the leaves rustle[2] in the gentle breeze,

Looking at them makes the eyes soothingly please.

It's a place holding special importance for any village,

Where the social and health workers in the grassroots work in linkage[3],

Unifying health, nutrition and sanitation in one passage,

Playing a crucial role in overcoming any damage.

It's still our Nation's glimmer[4] of hope in the outreach,

Where the availability to guide folks is beyond reach,

Hard to believe time and again countless barriers they breach,

So, time has ripened[5] to recognize their triumphs without any glitch.

....

[1] *walk in a leisurely way*

[2] *sound of leaves*

[3] *correlation*

[4] *shining faintly with a wavering light*

[5] *matured*

4. An Ode to the Unexplored Land

Amidst[1] the forests of *Dandakaranya*[2] where the *Bastar* stands apart,

The tribes of *Halbi, Gond, Marias*[3] and many more form its heart,

Divided by languages but united by rich heritage through its art,

Yet this precious entity's complete exploration hasn't been given a start.

From the deep valleys of *Keshkal*[4] to the calming waters of *Indravati*,

The presence of *Maa Danteshwari Temple*[5] cusps its divinity,

Though the long-standing Naxalism tends to plague[6] its integrity,

But the folks have fought tooth and nail to
preserve their own identity.

Beyond the geographical richness, some more
things mark it very special,

Numerous *Ram Van Gaman spots*[7] of the
Ramayana make it so historical,

And the aura of its *Palace*[8] and *Dussehra*[9] is
really mercurial,

Breaking all barriers, the way it has kept its
spirits high looks so surreal.

....

[1] *in between*

[2] *name of a forest mentioned in the ancient Indian epic
Ramayana*

[3] *local tribes*

[4] *name of a valley*

[5] *one of the Shakti Pithas*

[6] *cause continual trouble*

7 the path that Lord Rama, Sita and Lakshmana took during their exile years

8 The Bastar Palace

9 The Bastar Dussehra festival

5. Our Nation's Sorrow

So, we are approaching almost eight decades
of independence,

Well, can we really claim this fact with
absolute confidence?

With the caste and communal fights rising in
abundance,

Leaving our Nation to boil beyond the zenith[1]
with each filthy incidence.

Cries of women echoing in every nook and
corner are becoming a feature,

Seems everyone has turned their backs on
every torture,

Millions of youths facing the storm of
unemployment with a dark future,

Concrete jungles are proving to be a
double-edged sword for human creature.

Hopes still galore[2] as the countrymen stand in
the ruining tower,

With a ray of hope that their buzz would
shake up the peeps in power,

One day their voice will be listened to by
some superpower,

Patience and determination to bring about a
change is the need of the hour.

....

[1] *highest point*

[2] *in abundance*

6. Misery of Our Farmers

Climate has been their best friend since the
Stone Age,

But its recurring betrayal is pushing them
into a cage,

Despite their sheer[1] hard work, they are losing
the stage,

Facing a flurry of losses, they entangle deep
into a maze[2].

As their debts rise and mount beyond
imagination,

They feel life's becoming a surplus of
agonising[3] tension,

Slowly pushing their minds into the
doldrums[4] of negative action,

Seeing no options left they decide to leave
this world in frustration.

And so this cycle continues and the loss of
their lives becomes a trend,

Their families are ruined as they have no
penny left to spend,

Now, the only request to the rulers in power
is just stop to pretend,

Putting an end to the long-standing misery by
attempting to mend.

....

[1] *complete*

[2] *a network of paths and hedges*

[3] *painful*

[4] *depression*

7. An Innocence Stolen Away

Joy flows aplenty as a child is born into a family,

Slowly they crawl through their life's stages happily,

When their innocence see things with clarity and jovially,

That's the age to enjoy every moment joyfully.

Alas! But that's not the case with everyone though,

Many fall into the marital trap without their consensual[1] flow,

Suffering an everlasting and devastating[2] mental blow,

Ending their happy-go-lucky period and facial glow.

Voices raised many against such cultural
malpractices,

But everyone's silenced in the name of myths
and prevailing malices[3],

The time has come to put an end to such utter
nuisances[4],

By which saved will be many lives and more
horrific incidences.

....

[1] *agreeing*

[2] *highly destructive or damaging*

[3] *the desire to harm someone*

[4] *a person or thing causing inconvenience or annoyance*

8. March to the Urban Jungle

Yes, to the ones born in the village, life's so truly awesome,

Yet they are forced to leave their birthplace for more monetary[1] outcome,

To march miles to the cities with their families is so cruelsome,

On reaching, they learn that earning a daily bread is more of a burdensome.

Then they begin their new life with struggles all around,

In a whisker[2] their life seems to have taken a huge turnaround,

From walking the village streets to adjusting to the bustling[3] city background,

Slowly they start adapting for their livelihood
amidst the city compound.

And then this cycle continues for days,
months and years,

To make the future of the next generations
filled with cheers,

So that they put an end to their familial
problems and tears,

Thus, paving the way to travel back to native
villages sans[4] any fears.

....

[1] *financial*

[2] *a very small amount*

[3] *full of activity*

[4] *without*

9. Vanishing of the Abundant

It's a fact that our Earth's two-thirds is just water,

Yet we hear the cries of its scarcity every hereafter,

Ruining many lives for which the families slowly falter,

The so-called development is just causing the damage faster.

Roads, storeys and dams are made to fulfil all human needs,

Unknowingly hampering nature by all the careless deeds,

Some flooding, while some facing drought for all the greeds,

None know its harmful impact as there aren't
any leads.

All activities are stumbling[1] our natural water
resources in haste,

Endangering the life of water bodies with
some turning into waste,

The time has come to recharge the water table
by groundwater harvest,

Let's all raise our voices against the nuisance[2]
at the soonest.

....

[1] *losing balance*

[2] *a person or thing causing inconvenience or annoyance*

10. The Lost Sojourn of Train Journeys

A ride on the train that once brought cheer
has become a thing of the past,

Everyone's scared to think of who's going to
hold the dipping mast[1],

With the mishaps occurring here and there
way too fast,

People's grief and sorrow for losing their
loved ones is just so vast.

As the wagon[2] rolls along quickly on the
railway track,

That melody of moving fishplates[3] seems to
have taken a step back,

The heart fills with concerning thoughts
wondering if there's some crack,

Calling the Almighty for reaching the safe
shores seems to be the final hack.

Let's not lose all hope based on the rising
crisis all around,

There's always a light at the end of the tunnel
for a turnaround,

Keeping the fingers crossed for fighting back
to win the lost ground,

In a hope that our leaders will make our
journeys profound[4].

....

[1] *supporting pole*

[2] *bogie of a train*

[3] *a metal plate connecting two rails*

[4] *great*

11. A Meal to Savour

The bell rings with the clock striking two,

The children running around the corridors
without a clue,

With shining plates and hungry eyes, they
stand in a queue,

They wait for their turn for a meal of love and
care which is their due.

Sitting in rows they gossip around as they
continue their meal,

For many that's the reason for coming to
school with zeal[1],

With a ray of hope that through this food the
hunger will heal,

It's a scheme that's serving our Nation a great
deal.

It's much of a success in the way it has been
panned out,

But there's still scope for improvement
without a doubt,

Against anyone who tampers its quality, just
stand and shout,

That's the way to preserve its sanctity[2]
throughout.

....

[1] *enthusiasm*

[2] *purity*

12. Let's Bring Back the Glory Days!

Gone are the days when we waited for the clock to strike five,

So we could rush outdoors to play with our friends and dive,

Enjoying each moment without letting any complexity thrive[1],

Those were the golden days for which we still strive[2].

With the present era being that of over-digitalization,

Causing our next-gen to fall to its prey like an addiction,

The way it's hampering them mentally is beyond imagination.

Is this the outcome of the so-called urbanisation?

Seems high time we take note of this situation
as it's very strange,

Before it's too late and the control goes
beyond our range,

Thus, saving many lives from any irreversible[3]
change,

Paving the way for a healthy social exchange.

....

[1] *develop*

[2] *try hard*

[3] *that cannot be reversed*

13. Reviving the Morality

As the world moves faster, aren't we slowing
on moral values?

By forgetting the behavioural boundaries and
eternal[1] virtues,

Folks seem to lose their integrity in the
worldly blues[2],

Downing their companions to stamp their
authority and causing issues.

It's the person's attitude that matters more
than the degree,

That's the fact to which everyone does agree,

A society enriched with morality feels lively
and free,

It takes some great effort to grow an ethical[3]
tree.

Hampering one's self-respect in any situation
is not the right choice,

But there's every right for the people to raise
their voice,

Against all the proceedings by cutting down
the external noise,

Let's contribute in making a safe world where
the folks may rejoice[4].

....

1 long-lasting

2 sad feelings

3 moral principles

4 feeling of great joy

14. Life's a Game of Cricket

Life's a game of cricket where everyone's
playing their role in a certain way,

Combating all the swings and turns by
keeping them at bay,

Confidently ducking[1] all the bouncers[2]
without falling prey,

Running fast to chase their dreams amidst
any grey.

It's not the case that you can hit sixes for fun,

Just like the weather, the things in life will
surely take a turn,

Grinding[3] it out is the best option by opting
to play on,

While clawing[4] back to reclaim the lost
ground head on.

Opportunities come and go, but we need to
take a chance for success,

Reviewing to choose the best option forms an
important part of the process,

Always consulting the beloved team members
to avoid any mess,

That's the ultimate way to win any situation
without much distress.

....

[1] *bend down*

[2] *fast rising ball in cricket*

[3] *fight one's way out*

[4] *to move ahead slowly*

15. Overcoming the Myths

Since long the chains continue to exist,

The so-called casteism soars high without any resist,

Scaring the society by clenching[1] its wrist,

Many have struggled to resolve the twist.

Few preachers[2] show no mercy to the ones below them,

With some torturing them in every aspect causing mayhem[3],

Crushing the poor and marginalized[4] for which many do condemn[5],

Discrimination and humiliation of the lowly is still prevailing in tandem[6].

Still, the time's not up, so let's step ahead for resurrection[7],

To lead by example against all odds for societal correction,

By burying the deep ghosts of caste discrimination,

Let's march forward to build a healthy Nation.

....

[1] *grasp firmly*

[2] *a person delivering something publicly on caste or religion*

[3] *chaos*

[4] *low caste*

[5] *express complete disapproval of*

[6] *at the same time*

[7] *restoration*

16. Whispers of the Unheard

For centuries have they dwelled in the forest depth,

Defying all odds they have gained more strength,

For ages, they have been nature's precious wealth,

Efforts are made to enable them a calm breath.

Still, many think of leading a city life as a distant dream,

Sweating hard to resolve the daily woes[1] with no scream,

But working together with their fellows like a team,

To rise high towards the zenith[2] against any downstream.

Despite all the progress, many are still left behind,

Who just deserve a mere push of some kind,

For turning their dreams into reality with a grind[3],

So that the world soon gets many a precious find.

....

[1] *problems*

[2] *highest point*

[3] *fight one's way out*

17. Empowering to be the Best

It's a real irony to put some existing facts in place,

One responsible for carrying a life in Her womb has no solace[1],

Striving[2] to prove herself at every point in life's burning furnace,

Her endless struggles through all these years is a real disgrace.

As time passes in this fast-moving world quickly,

Empowering Her to be at par with the counterparts happily,

For to burn the candle of a healthy society steadily,

Defying the barriers to Her progress fiercely.

Small steps will definitely lead to the ultimate glory,

When the world stops treating Her sorely,

With Her achievements becoming a success story,

That's the way we can burn all the societal woes[3] without a worry.

....

[1] *comfort in the time of need*

[2] *trying hard*

[3] *problems*

18. When Home's a Battle Field

Behind every smiling home there's always a
residing pain,

Where the members fight amongst themselves
to look for their own gain,

But by doing this do they really know what
they finally attain?

Their children face the wrath[1] of everything
and cry in disdain.

An air of anguish[2], mistrust and revenge flows
through the house,

Trying to upstage each other like a game of
cat and mouse,

With some causing severe physical harm to
their spouse,

That's the sad reality of our society whether
they live in a hut or penthouse[3].

But such sensitive issues can't simply be swept
under the carpet,

What's the point in creating chaos in the
family like a fish market?

Eliminating these petty issues should be
everyone's target,

Making our society shine bright like a scarlet[4].

....

[1] *anger*

[2] *be extremely distressed about something*

[3] *a luxury apartment on the roof of a building*

[4] *brilliant red colour*

19. The Ageing Treasure

Yes, they have grown old but don't forget they are gold,

For their life experiences have a special hold,

Throughout their lives, they have been strong and bold,

That's the reality they have never told.

Sometimes they might sound to you harsh,

But they won't ever push you to get any scars,

Neither will they leave your hand if you get stuck in a marsh[1],

To them, you are still their little child gazing[2] at the stars.

Supporting them in their need fills their hearts with great pride,

While the opposite makes their feelings go downslide,

Leaving them to ponder where they took a wrong stride,

So, let's shoulder their responsibilities by being their supporting guide.

....

¹ *waterlogged land*

² *looking in a fixed direction*

20. The Unsung Saviours

With love and compassion[1] have they served
the people for ages,

Without worrying about the amount of
money they are paid as wages,

Reviving innumerable patients approaching
them at various stages,

Courageously weathering[2] every storm and
outrages[3].

From the grassroots to the city hospitals, they
render treatment promptly[4],

The midwives, nurses and doctors all work in
unison calmly,

Whether it's day or night they lend their
hands fondly[5],

While dealing with the ever-rising
shortcomings[6] smartly.

But their security becoming a concern with
the increased violence,

The ones harming their integrity should show
some common sense,

As their contribution to the society is
invaluably immense,

Any mistreatment towards them should be
severely punished as it's a serious offense.

....

[1] *concern for the sufferings or misfortunes of others*

[2] *come safely through*

[3] *an extremely strong reaction of anger*

[4] *immediately*

[5] *with affection*

[6] *failures to meet a certain standard*

21. Beyond Words and Promises

The depth of any relationship lies in its trust
and understanding,

Failure to which leaves the folks aloof[1] and
stranding[2],

Accepting each other's imperfections makes it
outstanding,

While focusing on the strengths makes it
more commanding.

And the smile flows all around as we stay
united,

Igniting a fire of jealousy among the ones who
have hatred,

Ignoring the unworldly ones and remaining
unaffected,

Living life to the fullest with our dearest
mates keeps us excited.

When friends become families it's truly
magnificent,

Where the freedom to express just becomes
proficient[3],

Whether happy or sad, the emotions remain
persistent,

So rather than having many, a circle of the
closest ones is sufficient.

....

[1] *unapproachable*

[2] *leaving someone without any option to move anywhere*

[3] *expert*